Compass Point

Phonics Readers

Race to a Fire!

by Rachel Mann

Reading Consultant: Wiley Blevins, M.A.
Phonics/Early Reading Specialist

 COMPASS POINT BOOKS

Minneapolis, Minnesota

Compass Point Books
3109 West 50th Street, #115
Minneapolis, MN 55410

Visit Compass Point Books on the Internet at *www.compasspointbooks.com*
or e-mail your request to *custserv@compasspointbooks.com*

Photographs ©: Cover: Corbis/First Light, p. 1: Corbis/First Light,
p. 6: left: Bruce Coleman Inc./Sarah Cotter, p. 6: right: Worldfoto/Paul A. Souders,
p. 7: Capstone Press/Gary Sundermeyer, p. 8: Capstone Press/Gary Sundermeyer,
p. 9: Bruce Coleman, Inc./Norman Owen Tomalin, p. 10: Worldfoto/Paul A. Souders,
p. 11: Worldfoto/Paul A. Souders, p. 12: 911 Pictures/Dave Radomski

Editorial Development: Alice Dickstein, Alice Boynton
Photo Researcher: Wanda Winch
Design/Page Production: Silver Editions, Inc.

Library of Congress Cataloging-in-Publication Data
Mann, Rachel, 1975-
  Race to a fire! / by Rachel Mann.
    p. cm. — (Compass Point phonics readers)
  Summary: Shows firefighters rushing to a store fire in an easy-to-read
text that incorporates phonics instruction and rebuses.
Includes bibliographical references and index.
  ISBN 0-7565-0522-4 (hardcover : alk. paper)
  1. Fire extinction—Juvenile literature. 2. Reading—Phonetic
method—Juvenile literature. 3. English language—Phonetics—Juvenile
literature. [1. Fire fighters. 2. Fire extinction. 3. Reading—Phonetic
method. 4. Rebuses.] I. Title. II. Series.
  TH9148.M26 2004
  628.9'25—dc21   2003006367

Table of Contents

Dear Parent or Caregiver,

Welcome to Compass Point Phonics Readers, books of information for young children. Each book concentrates on specific phonic sounds and words commonly found in beginning reading materials. Featuring eye-catching photographs, every book explores a single science or social studies concept that is sure to grab a child's interest.

So snuggle up with your child, and let's begin. Start by reading aloud the Mother Goose nursery rhyme on the next page. As you read, stress the words in dark type. These are the words that contain the phonic sounds featured in this book. After several readings, pause before the rhyming words, and let your child chime in.

Now let's read *Race to a Fire!* If your child is a beginning reader, have him or her first read it silently. Then ask your child to read it aloud. For children who are not yet reading, read the book aloud as you run your finger under the words. Ask your child to imitate, or "echo," what he or she has just heard.

Discussing the book's content with your child:
Explain to your child that smoke pouring out of a building usually means that there are flames inside. You may not see these flames from the outside. The firefighters wear protective helmets, coats, and pants so that the fire and smoke will not harm them.

At the back of the book is a fun Word Bingo game. Your child will take pride in demonstrating his or her mastery of the phonic sounds and the high-frequency words.

Enjoy Compass Point Phonics Readers and watch your child read and learn!

My Dame

My **dame** has a **lame, tame crane,**
My **dame** has a **crane** that is **lame.**
Pray, gentle **Jane,** let my
  dame's tame crane
Feed and come **home** again.

A  store is on fire.
Who will help?

Brave firefighters will help!
They can save it.

Grab a hat and  coat.
Race to the pole.

Hop on a red  fire engine .
Drive fast to the blaze.

Smell the smoke!
Go up the ladder.

Use a fire hose.
Wet the hot flames.

The fire is out.
The heroes save the !

Word List

Final *e*
blaze
brave
drive
fire
flames
hose
pole
race
save
smoke
use

r-Blends
brave
drive
grab

High-Frequency
go
look
out
to

Social Studies
firefighters
heroes
store

Read More

Freeman, Marcia S. *Fire Engines*. Mankato, Minn.: Pebble Books, 1999.

Raatma, Lucia. *Fire Fighters*. Community Workers Series. Minneapolis, Minn.: Compass Point Books, 2000.

Shaefer, Lola M. *Fire Station*. Who Works Here? Series. Chicago, Ill.: Heinemann Library, 2001.

Subois, Muriel L. *Out and About at the Fire Station*. Minneapolis, Minn.: Picture Window Books, 2003.

Index